In the Ordinary of my Life

In the Ordinary of my Life

Poems by
Augusto Manke

First published in 2020 by Annalese Press
134 Towngate
Netherthong
Holmfirth
West Yorkshire HD9 3XZ
England

Copyright © 2020 Augusto Manke

All rights reserved. No part of this publication may
be reproduced, stored, or transmitted in any form,
or by any means electronic, mechanical or photo-
copying, recording or otherwise, without the express
written permission of the publisher.

Cover design by Peter Wadsworth

British Library Cataloguing-in-Publication Data
A catalogue record for this book is available on
request from the British Library.

ISBN-978-1-9163620-1-7

For Angelo
miss you bro

Contents

We told we bein punks	1
Back then we pledged allegiance	3
Mama dishin up grits	5
Been thinkin about Stevie lately	8
We been livin in the projects	10
Mama always been church goin	14
Mama says my mission	17
Muskrat smashes windows	19
My mama tells Loretta and me	21
We tryin to survive	22
Got friends dealin	23
In the ordinary of my life	24
Girl down on the second floor	26
That wiry dog cross the street	28
One day here, next day gone	30
Loretta says I be cursin my fate	32
The song say	34
We countin days	35

Birdie, the brightest kid I know	37
Lately been doin somethin	39
I need to tell you	41
My mama don't curse fate	44

We told we bein *punks*

whatever that means
but then Leroy some devil
when it comes to eggin us on
shinin that piece of shit black stiletto
thinkin he soooo cool, sooo cool
and none of us cursin so much
as tryin to keep the lid on
and Stevie in the car sayin
Let's go, let's go man

and I'm tellin you I nearly
lost my temper
and you know what that look like
but Little Billie there
me supposed to be some sort of uncle
so I keep my cool, grab Billie
and get into the goddamn car

and Stevie guns the gas, drives off
before Gus can sink his jerk
into us.

Hell of a night.
got Billie home first
before the real ruckus set in
J.R. off at the Rumpus Grill
havin himself a good ol time
my mama on the outs with my dad.
So many hot chicks at the Rumpus
nearly wet my pants
and Stevie saying *Lookee
she's pussying up to you*
I don't see that
but I'm willin, I'm willin.
Keep sayin that to the world –
I'm willin……I'm willin
just not sure anybody listenin.

Back then we pledged allegiance

to the flag
in class, assembly
walked single file
bright as parrots

were told to take hold
memorize names, facts
countries.

All my life been on a high wire
about to fall
about to be saved

been playin hooky
mindin my own sort of manners
as if someday they gonna
matter.

Inside my heart
an unruly catfish
squirmin.

Mama dishin up grits

for breakfast
keeps tellin me *you better behave*
you want somethin out of this world
but what do she know
she never done it
cept one hijack outa here to Chicago
years ago when she left the old man
five months later come back
says the ice and wind whipped her
say he gone done treatment
worth another chance.
Now see where that's got her.

But this mornin
she in a good mood, spoonin up grits
in her short fuchsia bathrobe
my old man tellin her
your legs look hot, honey
then shovelin the grits in his mouth.

She's wearin a black curly wig
wears them cos her hair still thin
growin back after the chemo.
Tells me she's massagin her head
girlfriend Mico gave her some kinda oil
makes it grow back thick and faster
not sure I believe that.
The wigs change -
shiny brown bob with bangs
long and bleached as baked summer
pixie redhead

you never know day to day what you got
who she gonna be, shimmyin
into her one piece spangle pantsuit
next day short skirt and white boots.

Sometimes not sure she my mama
not just some sister or friend.

Never gonna see me grow old in this shithole tells me
as she slides out the door with her friends
heads down to the Halo dance club.
Old man left alone with the TV, his beer
and not even me cause I headin out.
No busy work, reruns gonna keep me
nailed to a tomb.

Been thinkin about Stevie lately

his time in the clinker for breakin into that house.
Damn fool!
Told him he gonna get himself in a shitload
of trouble, but when does he listen.
Been livin at his Aunt Blanche's place
sleepin nights on her couch last couple years
since his brother got caught trafficking crack.
Dumb shit brother.
Their mama cried three days
when the cops nabbed him
nearly got herself a heart attack.
Ungrateful bastard!
Vinnie was the oldest
shoulda known better.
Their mama scrapin by on disability
havin to hobble out in the street with her walker
collect empty cans, bottles.

Stevie say the whole place fallin apart
says once Vinnie gone she had to take in
some lodger to cover the bills.
He now livin at his Aunt Blanche's
over past Dickson, and she no piece of cake
what with the guys she brings home
hopin to find a husband.
Vinnie locked away, tagged with a record.
Stevie lucky to get a job sweepin streets
at the rate he goin.

Some days I wake up
not sure whether to feel cursed or grateful
this life I been handed
watchin my friends eat crushed bread
blacken their hearts
in the soot we be walkin.

We been livin in the projects

more years than I remember
paper thin walls
listenin to scream fits
being called *punks*
flickin our matches
outside on the concrete
the stairwells smellin of sick
the way they cut maintenance
save costs.

Mama always remindin me –
this is temporary, babies
just till we get ourselves up on our feet
and your daddy get that promotion
to office he be waitin on.
That was seven years ago.
No promotion happen.
The old man still on the floor
in the bottle factory, gainin weight

smokin more cigarettes
come home dog tired and headin
over to the TV or pool hall.
Mama still takin the bus uptown
to do fancy ladies' nails
as if they got themselves cocktail parties
weekend mansions
Mama with her wig, knee high boots
toothy smile -
I tell them what they want to hear, honey
make um laugh
show um pictures of you and Loretta
in your Halloween costume, 4th grade
remember that babies —
she tell us at the supper table.

Remember Augusto you was a spider man
and Loretta a lady bug with big glitter antenna.
They love it. Love knowin bout your lives.

Get myself really good tips.
And they always come back.

That's my mama
with her flamin grin
able to conjure the world
make a rat into a rabbit
make our past seem like apple fritter
an American flag flappin.

Get sick of hearin it all
but know it's the fantasy she live by.
Like my old man's pool hall
and dreams of a big truck, promotion
the way my sister kissin up to every boy
my mama imaginin her life as perfume
glitter gowns, singin copy of Diana Ross
on a world tour.

Some days don't want to head anywhere
my world seems flat
a thin razor of truth
and I'm not willin, not willin.
That why I write in here.
Try to make some sense, keep my sanity.
Tell myself there's somethin more.

Mama always been church goin

but not my old man.
Says god let him down years ago
when he needed a place to live, new shoes
no one come callin.
His mama slavin with five kids
and no man
says all they ate was fried spam, potato
till he could barely use a fork.

Mama say he's a conversion waiting to happen
that one day he gonna walk over hot coals
shout Jesus.
I've been listenin to this for years.
My sister and I dragged into church
with our slicked down hair, Goodwill clothes
black patent shoes

been listenin to the Hallelujah chorus
folks raisin up their hands *praise Jesus*
bein born again, speakin in tongues
watchin them coo with my mama
till I grown old enough to be left behind find
my own way to heaven, thank you

not seein any kinda promise on the horizon
Loretta shimmyin her hips
in those paper thin dresses
mama with her assortment of wigs

the old man chuckin his beer cans after work
watchin old reruns

findin my own way.
Not sure what that be -

a troubled field gone brown
or the ache of the earth
tremblin?

Mama say my mission

to be a good man
decent son
as if my life a water pitcher
and everybody want a splash

but me
I feel more a hub cap
tumbleweed
spinnin down the road
as if Armageddon follow
my greasy hair
crap old high tops
the way I primp up big
as if I can save things
meanwhile feel like nothin
in a sea of debris.

Tell me – who gonna come for me
when the night max out

when my friends drive by
with their gold bracelets
fancy watches, cell phones
tempt me

who gonna show me a different season
tell me I'm not just some son of a bitch
loser?

Muscrat smashes windows

with his fist
Leroy collects chains, leather gloves
keeps um in his trunk just in case
Mossy got his hands in acid
gonna make nothin
of their life's metal
they not careful.

I been stringin my time
tryin to keep my head above water
cause jail time don't sound profitable
cause my folks been through enough
without me causin more.

Don't mean I'm on the fast track
ever been teacher's pet, prize peacock

just amounts to walkin the shadows
tryin not to get myself eaten
end up a bloodbath.

My mama tells Loretta and me

be a spoon of honey with folks
cos we all need it
as if this city not a heap of bandages
the world in revolt

I have hard words to say
bout where we headin
what we done

but then might as well
spit drool outa my mouth
as much as anybody gonna listen.

Can mercy get us outa here
avert disaster
set us up in a house
buy groceries
get my mama better pay
my old man a job beyond
backbreakin?

We tryin to survive

Stevie, Billie, Victor R.
even Diablo who got a maniac temper
and gonna be lucky to make it to twenty-one.

Mama want me to go back
get my GED
say I gonna need it.

Been stayin out late.
Cruisin in Stevie's car.
Half lookin for trouble.
Half lookin for somethin else.

Not even sure what that be.

Got friends dealin

findin a way to charm their wallets
showin me hundred dollar bills
say just five hours a night
a tight mouth, right talk
gonna get me someplace.

Know Victor broke both arms
of that guy over on Madison
when he wouldn't pay up
says they gave him a bunch of chances
but louse bag
deserves what he got.

Been tryin to stay away
meanwhile pockets empty.
Afraid of that shit
what it does, doesn't do
way it gets hold of folks
strangles.

In the ordinary of my life

I eat toast, scrambled egg
pool them in ketchup
folks come and go
grumble bout the shitty weather.
I leak your name out of the salt shaker
make you a flawless mound
then fallen mess.

In the ordinary of my life
cockroaches parade
parish the kitchen
the kid downstairs kicks the dirt aimless
I pull up to the dark in my bat car
say – *hey bro what's happenin*
hear about torn limbs
the downsized tire factory
Sully neighborhood gone hipster
acid and pistols.

You poke holes in the dark
stalk death, loss
the lonely boy down the hall in 4A.
His mama's mouth is a bruise mark.

Girl down on the second floor

got herself into college.
Some big fancy one in Massachusetts.
Everybody talkin about it.
She keeps to herself
plays with nobody
her mama work two, three jobs
dad died of some kinda cancer.

Her name is Millita
has mousy hair, always looks pale, thin
as if nobody feed her
as if sunlight missin
too much indoors and a ghost suckin.

My mama throw in my face
about she gonna amount to somethin
bring home the bread
while the rest of us stew and wait.

Not holdin my breath.
Know that college no guarantee.
Could be rest of her life
she'll have to work a ton of hours
be strapped to a screen, debt

stay pale, indoors
that having promise
no guarantee
things happen
your pa gets cancer
brother becomes a drug addict
every teacher you thought you loved
hates you.

That wiry dog cross the street

isn't comin back anytime soon
got swiped by a car five days ago
when old Mrs. Pauley dropped the leash
the dog rushed into the road.

Got to admit the old lady's eyesight poor
goes down her steps huggin the rail
struggles with her wire food cart
to keep the wheels straight.

The wiry dog cross the street
not young, not old
somewhere in-between
had a *yap yap yap* that really annoys

other times could roll over
on its belly
melt any neighbor.

Know for a fact the old lady spoilt
the hell outa the dog
bought bones from the butcher
a red check coat come winter
now has her window blinds shut
not answerin the door.

Wonder what we do
about loss
a world turned weary.

One day here, next day gone

that's what happened to Elroy's grandpa.
Saw him haulin bags of groceries
just last week
now he bein dug in the ground.
How that happen.
Nice man. Always had a smile for me
say – *hey, boy, how ya doin*
every time we pass.

How that happen.
Fast as flick of a matchstick.
Here one minute, gone the next.
I twenty-one.
Just startin some kind of life.
Don't even know yet what it look like
where I headed
who gonna be travelin with me.

Mama say —
Whatever else you do
you better bring Jesus
since I been a kid she say that.
Brought Jesus when the old man doin drugs
brought Jesus with her breast cancer
as if some hallelujah chorus gonna save.
All I know is I got a stockpile of winter
no GED, no big forecast future
that if Jesus on my tail
he hidin somewhere off a side street
gonna have to work his ass off
to find me.

Loretta say I be cursin my fate

but it still gonna carry me
so I better decide what I doin
and quick.

And who she to get so smart.
Just sixteen and tellin me she gonna
get into some community college
become a dental hygienist
earn lots of bucks
get her crooked teeth fixed

as if scrapin a pic inside rich folks' mouths
makin teeth pearly
gonna make her sing
offer up a car, fancy handbags

while the world sinkin
fast as I speak
and most of us blindfolded

just sweatin the rent
polishin our words
bright as candy.

The song say

I got the world on a string
sitting on a rainbow
got the string round my finger
what a world, what a life
but it not bein sung for me
for somebody else.

I look through the ink black dark
its bullet holes, pup tents
swear the stars been blinded
the street on a diet of pistols

want to get things straight
come clear
be more than a gold ring
sugar words
some rainbow cussing.

Tell me –
life different for you than me?

We countin days

till mama gets her license
never had a car in this place
never able to just take off
cruise out of here like big shots.
Mama been savin
says we gettin a shiny red Buick
used one from her friend's old man
already put down a deposit
black cloth seats, stereo radio
says we all goin for a joy ride
soon as she passes the test.

My old man half jealous
claims we all lazy, not satisfied
with what we already got.

My mama making plans
Cruise City, Johnson Beach
amusement park

say she and her girlfriends
gonna soak their bodies, beach tan.

I admit – half jealous.
Got no money for meals
no prospects.
Diggin   diggin   diggin
see where I am
where I goin
what I don't want to be
who I might become.

Birdie, the brightest kid I know

done got himself shot the other day.
Nobody saw it comin, least of all me.
Just walkin his sweet ass Jesus body
down Pine Street past the drug store
on way to buy dozen eggs for his mama
when black sedan pulls up
shatters the glass window
riddles his body in a sea of bullets.

Everybody say they got the wrong boy
not who they thought
but what good that do Birdie
smartest kid in my class
skinny guy who never said much
old man run off
mama raised him
works teller at some bank.
Birdie gone. Senseless.
That's the crap that happens here.

Step out your door, take your life
in your hands
gotta keep your eyeballs turned
in all directions

else you be a target, somebody's
blood red revenge
quick trigger.

Nobody got sense when it comes
to guns.

Lately been doin something

don't want to do
studyin to get my GED.
Birthday gift for my mama
cause she keeps beggin.
Doin it for her.
Not that it matter much
who gonna want me to shelve things
answer their sales calls.

Got no prospects for my future.
No idea what to become –
race car driver, punk, prizefighter
stuntman, detective
story writer, salesman
stake my life for a cause
no idea
but my mama a hug machine
under the tough cookie
half wanna make her proud.

Her birthday November 23th
and if all goes well I get that
piece of paper in a month
surprise her with somethin.
Watch her joy weep.

I need to tell you

I am more than you think –
some snot nosed kid married to winter
the one in soiled sneakers who shoots
ball
lives in a tenement, swear words his
nights
can't count good without a calculator
the one who gets tempted to riot
stomp on sissies
show everybody muscle

need to tell you
the world don't make sense
that in those crowded classrooms
my teachers saw only the crust of me
lost faith

that sometimes day feels like night
night feels like day

I get scared of where we headin
who we'll become
that maybe I'm more than a pistol
sewer grate
somethin more
a lullaby for the world's blisters

that somethin keeps tryin to break
through
this harsh wind
find a hold

that my mama still walks into her day
as if there are no assassins
just singin
has never lost faith
I need to tell you
that maybe deep down
I want to count for somethin

bigger than the world's arcades
that who I've been, where I come from
don't mean I'm a finished thing.

My mama don't curse fate

wears it like a pricy wristwatch
pink paneled summer
keeps her ocean
clean

won't call out monsters
squeeze the dark so hard
it bleeds.

Still autumn swings into winter
the heat runs stingy
my mama gets diagnosed with cancer
every hour of every day
I look through the keyhole
of her lips
see God offerin up
spoonfuls of hope
while I weep.

Augusto Manke works swing shift in a warehouse
in Illinois. He says he is still trying to figure out
his life,
has a few clues.

This is his first chapbook.

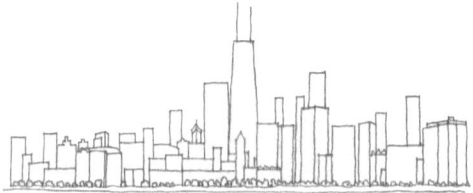

www.ingramcontent.com/pod-product-compliance
Lightning Source LLC
Chambersburg PA
CBHW021133080526
44587CB00012B/1265